MIDNIGHT PHILOSOPHIES

By Marricke Kofi GANE

Copyright © 2014 by Marricke Kofi Gane

MIDNIGHT PHILOSOPHIES

By Marricke Kofi Gane

ISBN: 978-1-909326-02-6

All rights reserved solely by the author. The author guarantees all contents are original and do not infringe upon the legal rights of any other person or work. No part of this book may be reproduced in any form without the permission of the author. For permission requests and others, write to the Author at:

author@marrickekofigane.com

Published by MarrickeGanePublishing

Distributed by Amazon

DEDICATION

To my father, Gershon, who taught me to think;
To my mother, Charity, who taught me reason;
To Rev Dr J. Nanjo, who taught me to live both.

Contents

INTRODUCTION	vii
AFRICA	1
POLITICS	15
LIFE	27
CHRISTIANITY	125

INTRODUCTION

This book is a compilation of thoughts and philosophies that have crept into my mind in my midnight hours. Some I have lived, others I barely fathom. Why they come to me, no man can explain – but perhaps because I sit at the pillars of my mind daily to open its gates.

For the purposes of solely making reading easier, I have used the male gender in this book to refer to all genders. I have also attempted to make reading easier by classifying my thoughts and philosophies under the headings Africa, Life, Politics and Christianity. There may be a few that could fall under more than one category – it only goes to prove "thought" is fluid.

A man ought to think and ask himself questions. He ought to think unhindered and question himself daily, for that is his greatest liberty and fulfilment – that he owns his own ideas and thoughts; that he can form reason which is acceptable to him and others.

If you agree on anything here said, this book has served its purpose. If you, on the other hand disagree with the contents herein, this book has served its purpose too – either way, you would have needed to search your own mind. That really is the goal.

Marricke K. Gane

AFRICA

FREEDOM

Is it true, the thing that I hear? – That Africa now has its freedom. Is that really so? How then is it, the rest of the world tells her what economic policies to use? Why is she told what types of governments to have; how her peoples must relate; how she ought to manage her resources; whether she has the right to defend her people the way the super-powers do; when to speak and not to speak; and what religious and ethnic alignments are right or wrong. Were these super-powers by themselves subject to these intrusions in their own democratic evolution? Why then must Africa sign up for them? Can someone tell me why?

THE POWERS THAT BE.....
THE VULNERABLE GET TOUCHED

The "powers that be" will not touch Syria because they know Russia is her friend and that the enemy of Russia's enemy is Russia's friend.

The "powers that be" will not touch Iran because they know suicide bombers will be on their doorsteps in the morning...

The "powers that be" will not touch Zimbabwe because they know their dark and dirty secrets; but besides that, because a lot of their capital is locked up in the lands of that country...

The "powers that be" will not touch China because she is both their lender and their industry sponsor...

The "powers that be" will not touch North Korea because she knows no diplomacy and her guns are pointed day and night towards the bedroom of these "powers"...

The "powers that be" will not touch the Saudis because they can turn off the oil tap for just one day and that could spell doomsday – one day...

The "powers that be" will not touch Israel because they possess economic and military intelligence second to none and are bearers of the Abrahamic covenants...

The big question is – Do the "powers that be" have a reason not to touch Ghana, my beloved country? Will they be endangering their own interest if they touched Ghana in a wrong way?

I really don't blame them. What do they have to fear? After all, we have baked bread of natural resources in our soil, yet we cannot stand on our independent feet except we are given dimes and pennies of sustenance. We have an educational system teaching our citizens purely imported knowledge, making them feel nothing of our own is good enough. We have lands, oil, timber and gold that are owned by everybody else but us... and on and on...

So YOU tell me, what is the threat we pose to the "powers that be"? Why should they be concerned about walking into our "bedrooms" and turning us on our own beds to face the position "THEY" want us to face? YOU tell me...

The "powers that be" cooperate with some people, and RULE over others. Watch all those they RULE over – they have one thing in common – they have NO bargaining chips.

THE WORLD IS A POKER TABLE

Some Countries OWN the casino

Some countries make the DEALS

Some countries PLAY the game

And my AFRICA sits at it with no bargaining chips.

LEAVE COLONIALISM ALONE, WILL YOU?

Some Africans say it is the slavery of bygone years that have held us back and I have asked: now that we are free men, what have we so far achieved and with what speed of urgency have we done so, to make up for time lost? In decades past, before we were enslaved, what did we achieve? Can somebody tell me why?

We have said the corruption of our leaders rob us of the continent's wealth; and I ask, if we had built banks like the Swiss, and pledged to protect the wealth of others, would they also have brought their countries' corruptly-gotten gains to us for safekeeping? Can someone please tell me why?

It is said wars and violence orchestrated by past colonial masters have taken away Africa's opportunities; and I ask:– if we were to put the same guns and mines in the hands of the children of our past masters, would they kill their own brothers, maim their sisters and slaughter their kindred? Someone, please, tell me why?

THE AFRICAN HEAD

I don't dispute that the African masses need a change in their mind-set. But here is the thing - the body is made up of the feet, the hands, the belly, the nose and all the other parts. Irrespective of their functions or location on the body, they MUST all follow and go where the BRAIN decides.

I agree people's mental attitude should change, but change to what? If we say their current mentality is not right; we must provide them the mentality that we think is RIGHT for them to follow. So we come back to the human body again. No other parts of the body will move together in any one direction unless the BRAIN figures it out first.

And if anyone cares to know, the brain, sits in the "Head" and the "Head" sits on top of the entire "Body".

They that have ears let them understand what I speak.

RECOVERING OUR LOST RECOVERIES

Africa is late, no doubt. It's exactly for this reason we cannot afford to thinking only about finding solutions to today's African problems. No. in fact, we ought to be thinking how to solve tomorrow's problems, both for Africa and the world at large. It's the only way we can cover grounds as a continent.

We have lagged so far behind that the only way to recover lost grounds is to buy uncharted grounds in the future, long before anyone else gets there.

LET'S THROW THE DICE AGAIN

Is it true, this thing that I hear? It is that violence in Africa has destabilized her efforts to become a better continent. Or so I have heard many argue – that the same colonial powers of old are to blame for these destabilizations. I wonder. How is it, that Africa blames the powers of old? How is it that in spite of Africa's diseases and hunger, she is still able to wield a gun and kill her own people? Or is it not the men of her own womb killing her children? I may be wrong to ask: if Africa were to put guns and land mines in the hands of the children of her colonial masters, would they slaughter their own brothers and sisters, mothers and fathers? Can someone please tell me why?

MADIBA! MANDELA!
A LIFE LIVED, A HOPE GIVEN....

On the bone of this day
Our chest we beat as men,
The tears of our women, an anguished flood.
Kings mourn, nations troubled, Heaven salutes.
Aye! The unborn listen from their mothers' wombs.
Madiba! Nkosi! Mandela is gone, yet Mandela lives.

On the bone of this day
Unjust bars that once bound you, twice humbled.
Aye! In their darkness, birthed humanity's great light.
Liberty, your life taught; freedom, your path defined.
A dream believed, a fight fought, a love lived.
Madiba! Nkosi! Mandela is gone, yet Mandela lives.

On the bone of this day
Africa! A mother lost at sea with her children,
Her beacon of light, her own son, a course lit to shore.
Aye! A towering hope, a milestone of strength.
Believe again Africa! Believe again humanity!
Madiba! Nkosi! Mandela is gone, yet Mandela lives.

On the bone of this day
Stare we, into the ages; defiance to death's cold grips,
Stands tall the world, a belief in humanity again
Rise bold our hearts, viva! May good always triumph.
Shout we Madiba! His light, glory; his hope, forever!
Madiba! Nkosi! Mandela is gone, yet Mandela Lives.

A BEGGAR'S GOLDEN BOWL

I am told that the continent of Africa has one of, if not, the richest concentrations and mix of natural and human resources, vast portions of the former which are still untapped. If Africa chose to, could she live without needing to depend on the world? Could the world live without the resources of Africa? Doesn't she who bakes the bread set the price? So how is it that the resources of Africa are not priced by Africa? How is it that in so many cases the resources of Africa are not even owned by Africa? Why is it that with all her vast deposits of natural resources, Africa still holds out her begging bowl, moulded in gold and begging for quarters, dimes and pennies? Can someone please tell me why?

WHEN DEFIANCE BECOMES THE REAL FREEDOM

I am told, that Africa should make an effort to learn democracy and good governance from the "more developed" countries. I have often wondered why. Surely, there must have been a time when these "developed" countries were undeveloped, and at the time when they were in this state, did they practice the same "democracy and good governance" that they now beseech Africa to employ? So what exactly defines a developed or underdeveloped nation? Is it the paved roads or the speed with which a nation hurries to reach the end of time, or the proliferation of nature's destruction? Is it the extent to which a nation dilutes its own identity and culture or the profundity of its striving to consolidate power and rule over others? Indeed, I too must ask, is democracy the only way for Africa's evolution? Should it, of necessity, operate in a like manner because it has worked for the developed countries who preach its rightness? Who influenced their evolutions? Why do "they" get to decide, seek to influence, or be the ones to determine the path of evolution Africa must follow? Why does Africa so willingly oblige by refusing to find the governance that works for her? Can someone please tell me why?

POLITICS

THE REAL AUTHORITY

Authority is not to for you to give an order and for another to take it.

Authority is not to act in arrogance over your fellow man.

It isn't to speak and receive silence in return or to enforce your will and receive total submission. Authority is being above other men and adding to them, what they need to rise above themselves.

After all, all men were created equal, but some, more than others.

If your fellow men cannot look up to heaven and be grateful for your existence, then you really haven't been in authority.

I have nothing to say about the kind of politics practiced in the era of my fathers.

DO NOT LORD IT OVER US

I fear a man who is in authority but under none himself. But I fear a man even more, who receives no advice from any other man.

I fear a man who knows all things; but I fear a man even more, who embraces ignorance.

I fear a man who will not learn from his mistakes, but I fear a man even more who will not try, and make a mistake trying.

I HAVE MY CONCERNS ABOUT OUR DEMOCRACIES

I have searched to understand the nature of our democracy. A deep mystery and paradox is all I have been left with. If there is anything I have come to understand, it is this truth: that our democracy is really a two-point working system of consenting control, where a pack of wolves hold a flock of sheep in a barn, opening the door for them to come out only when the latter need to be eaten.

(i) The electorate only feel they have POWER when given an opportunity at elections, to vote men into power and yet, feel POWERLESS to pull them down when they appear incapable of performing their duties.

(ii) Paradoxically, it is the men elected who give the electorate "THE OPPORTUNITY" (elections) to exercise their "perceived power" and without which their power is worthless. Knowing this, "the chosen ones" open opportunities (elections) for the masses to exercise their "power of APPROVAL" (which brings them into office) and intentionally SHUT the opportunities (referendums & votes of confidence) for the masses to exercise their "power of DISAPPROVAL" (which would take them out of office).

Isn't it amazing, that ALL POWER belong to the people when they are locked up behind the bars of "democracy", and yet the KEYS needed to open the gates for them to step out and freely exercise that power rests in the CLAWS of those over whom they ought to exercise such power.

You be the judge – OUR democracy is NOT for the people, it is for them that CONTROL the people. You don't take meat from wolves by asking them, you take it from them by………….

You decide.

DEMOCRATIC DICTATORSHIP = OUR DEMOCRACY

I had two dogs; one was named "Susu", which I trained to come close to me anytime I gave him the command. The other, I called "Follo", which I brought home at a later date. Follo was a quick learner and not long after, she started imitating the response I expected from Susu when I called him. But later, something extraordinary struck me. I realized there were times when I called Susu and he would choose not to come to me and at other times he would. Follo, on the other hand, always came when I called.

Then it dawned on me. Susu had LEARNED the commands out of choice and so he obeyed or disobeyed them out of choice. In other words, he had total control over when to respond or not. This was not done to disrespect me, it was simply Susu exercising his right to reason and act based on choice. Follo, on the other hand, was merely an imitator of the expected response, not understanding the basis or the genesis of the command. Follo did not know that following the command "come here" was based on choice rather than obligation. She did not know that the command was learnt and understood by Susu and not merely imitated. As a result, Follo had no alternative but to yield to the command. She did not know that the alternative to following the command existed – she did not have to follow it.

The command to "come here" is somewhat like DEMOCRACY. Susu represents the country with more than 80% literate citizens who understand that democracy is their choice and its strength depends on their exercising it. Follo represents the country with more than 60% illiterate citizens as the majority, whose only understanding of democracy is that politician give orders and citizens follow, anything in between is disobedience or disloyalty. Whether the order is given through policies or propaganda, they simply follow. Follo is the citizenry that believes that the strength of democracy lies in the politicians exercising it by making decisions solely on their behalf.

So you see - the word "DEMOCRACY" is one, but its practice is dual. There really is no such thing as true democracy in a country of illiterates. No, this is a democratic dictatorship shared by two political parties.

THE POLITICIAN'S CREED

The politicians of the world claim to feel the suffering of the people. If they really felt the pain of the people, they would be torn apart by the sheer magnitude of it. Jesus did, and his sweat turned to blood. Now, I ask you this - how can you feel my pain when my heart is in me and yours in you?

THIS REALLY IS POLITICS

STEALING: When what lawfully belongs to you is taken from you without your knowledge or consent!

CORRUPTION: When what lawfully belongs to you is taken from you with your encouragement, knowledge and wilful consent!

POLITRICKS

POLITRICKS = Mass deception and swindling of large herd of human sheep by a few greedy and broke human wolves.

But the mystery however is this – the wolves are not by themselves wolves. They are mere sheep who understand that sheep will always follow a command and, consequently, chose to be the givers and not the takers of the command.

LONELY AND COLD IS THE ROAD OF POWER

To walk in power is to walk the lonely road of great personal sacrifices.

It means to show no weaknesses in the midst of your greatest weakness;

It means to distrust at all times, even those you wish to trust most;

It means to share no intentions though it isolates a man from all humanness;

It means to live above all scrutiny, if it means living without the freedom of men;

It means to walk in every manner of confidence, facing your fears alone.

It means to stand away from the crowd and yet be the reason for the crowd.

This is Power – it is NOT for every man save the man who believes the good he can do with it.

IMITATORS OF POWER; RULERS IN HUMILITY

Image can be very distorting. For example, I know a man only by his daily life, but to know him better still, I ask his wife. I have seen men who profess to have power, yet begging for daily bread in the corridors of authority. Yet those who wield true power sit on thrones of humility, wielding the scepter of servitude.

Indeed, you only hear the rumbling of the belly when it is empty. The heaviness of knowledge weighs on the lips of a man and keeps him silent while he that lacks it also lacks a restraint over his tongue!

LIFE

THE WORLD SAYS IT IS ADVANCING – IS IT REALLY?

I find human beings interesting.

As the world advances in years, we have retrogressed in everything we're made of – emotions, relationships, our thinking and reasoning, values and, indeed, even our spirituality. Yet even now, we claim the advancement of the human race.

Our modern advances seem to be eroding all past achievements. We claim advances in knowledge, but the world economy is shattered. We claim advancement in science but still are yet to match the sciences used in building the pyramids of Egypt. Information technology has made the world a global village but we're blinded by how it tears apart the social interactions between humans.

Our souls have been traded for materiality and our spirits sold for the shadows of ungodly spirituality. Sad!

AGE

Age will take away my stubborn black hair and leave me grey. It may take away my smooth skin and leave me wrinkled. Age may even take away tomorrow and leave me only today, but the one thing I won't let it take away from me is the good memories. Today, as I have breath in me, I strive to create good memories because they will be my only companions tomorrow.

AGE IS JUST A NUMBER, THEY SAY

It saddens me when I hear people say age is nothing but a number. They forget that these numbers are the hands of life's clock - just as the day is the microsecond hand, a week is the seconds' hand; just as a month, is the minute hand and the years, the hour hand. Age is not just a number – it is THE number that tells how late or how early you are in life's journey.

TO DO IS TO HAVE ATTITUDE

I have never really understood this thing called "attitude" until now. It is simply made up of two sides of a coin – a decision to do something and doing it well. It takes a man far beyond the skies. Your "doing" no longer depends on anything except "your decision to do". That way, lack, circumstances, inequalities and limitations do not affect your "doing". That is "ATTITUDE". Here is my advice – do not expect a man to have "attitude" if he can neither make decisions nor act on them.

ALL THAT IS BEAUTIFUL

I haven't really understood the complexity of this thing called "beauty." To me, everything is beautiful, whose memory can bring me a smile, or sober me to say, "Surely, that's a good work of creation". Everything else is not ugly – they just haven't warmed my heart yet.

THE BEGINNING

The beginning of anything or any man always has inscribed in it how the end should be. If you wish to change the end, you need to go back to the beginning to change the order. The only problem is that many people go back to the beginning – and stay there.

BRAVERY - A BRIDGE UNKNOWN

Bravery is not that a man should face impossible situations from which others have turned away – after all if he triumphs, he will enjoy a reward for his daring. Bravery is found in the decision one makes to venture into the unknown, where there are no guarantees that it shall become known. Paradoxically, being brave is the only way, by which we can make known, that which was previously unknown. Thus, the making of such decisions become the bridges between the unknown and reality – now that, is bravery.

OF DISASTERS, CHANGES AND THE PARADOX

The world is changing fast, but the changes are slowing the world down. This is not a paradox – it's a disaster! But here is the paradox: the disaster is not in the fast changes and slowing world – it is in the truth that we, who run the world, neither understand the fast changes nor are willing to change to counter the world's slowing down. This, is not a disaster, it is a paradox.

TO LEARN IS TO UNLEARN

The hardest part of going forward is not really learning the new things. It is unlearning the old things that have kept us where we are. It is the old things we know, that usurp the thrones of the new things unknown. Nevertheless, every king will fight to keep his crown; and so it is, that the unprogressive things known will fight to keep its throne from the progressive things unknown.

TECHNOLOGY DEMANDS CHANGE

Imagine being on a fast-moving bus. The faster it moves, the faster you move too and the quicker you get to your final destination. Now imagine again a fast-moving bus, but this time around you are standing on the highway in its path, remembering that this bus does not stop for anything or anyone.

Technological know-how and information are becoming available and accessible at a phenomenal pace that demands that YOU are also moving fast- either at the same rate or faster. If you stand STILL, you will be CRUSHED… and I do mean CRUSHED!

MAKING YOUR MARK

Here are seven reasons why I believe you should seek to make an impact in the world:

The world is BIG enough for all of us to make an impact, to make a dent, to be celebrated and leave proud footprints in history for the generations after us.

(1) The world and history remember those who have solved some its problems or given it knowledge hitherto unknown, not passengers who just passed through.

(2) There are some levels of wealth that will only come to you as a result of the service you give and the impact you made on humanity.

(3) Making an impact in the whole world or some part of it is a major legacy to leave the generations yet unborn. It serves as a foundation of fame and world-acceptance from which they can launch their own destinies.

(4) Impacting the world is proof that you serve a creative, living God. Otherwise, how else can you prove that your God is great if you can't prove that it is His power in you that has enabled you to make an impact?

(5) Making an impact in your chosen area is the real fulfilment of your destiny. God does not create ineffective people. You'll only be fulfilled if what you live for is impacting a larger community than just you and your household, because only then does your life produce added value for every other life it makes happy. That's just how it is.

(6) Making an impact by using your own gift or calling is mostly the only way you can ensure that your voice is heard. In fact I believe it is the easiest way to ensure that your voice counts on matters you want to see changed because when you speak, your voice carries the approval of all those whom you have impacted.

(7) Making an impact, one way or the other, is really the only investment that never stops paying out handsome rewards beyond your own lifetime.

CHOICES, CHOICES, CHOICES,

Everything in life is the outcome of choices, whether they are choices made ourselves or those made on our behalf by virtue of our own willingness or negligence or whether they be made in response to or in anticipation of past or future events. They are all choices that each has its own sure consequence.

Indeed, not making a choice by itself is a choice. But the greatest of all, are the choices made when one stands face to face with the fruits of yesterday's choices: if they are good fruits we should choose to perpetuate goodness; and if they are bad fruits, to terminate the evil.

THE WILL TO YIELD, OR NOT TO YIELD

There is a grace, a mind and a spirit common to all men – its manifestation lies in the will of man! It is our only sovereign right – that we have a will to live, to stand for truth, to change, to love and to fight.

Whether we hated when we ought to have loved, whether we lied when we ought to have spoken truth, whether we folded our arms and stood back when we ought to have fought - it is all a choice in the exercise of our will.

But this thing I know is certain - that before the will of a man decides what he should do, his spirit tells him what is right, what is true and what needs to be done. If his will chooses to agree with his spirit, he is a strong man, if not, then surely the laziness of his will, surpasses a sloth's.

WHERE EXACTLY IS A "NEUTRAL POSITION?"

I have come to realize that there is no such thing as middle ground or neutrality in human society. At best, neutrality is just a state of transition. There will always only be two sides and you, abstaining from making a decision which to choose, only means you have elected to leave the realms of grace for grass – just like an undecided stone cannot be neutrally suspended in mid-air, but must fall to the grass below. If there was such a thing as neutrality, the law of gravity would cease to exist.

READ THE MOST TO DO THE MOST

I see two cities on either side of the river Jordan. On the one side, the city of expectations and on the other, fulfillment - the only bridge joining them together is knowledge. Those who read the most do the most, for they make a bridge between impossibilities and possibilities by binding a knot between hope and manifestation. They are like clouds. The more they read, the more they gather their minds as rain. A day comes when they have no choice but to fall heavily as showers of the brain – and the world will have no choice but to be soaked with them.

DISCERNMENT

To be sceptical is insanity, to be discerning is divine. Scepticism only throws away good opportunities because it reaches a decision, before it considers it fully. On the other hand, to be discerning is to hold your decision by the hand and walk it through the process of consideration. The truth is - many pay the price for discernment and are sold scepticism because the packaging is usually similar.

DUST TO DUST OR EARTH ON EARTH?

I sat in a park today, I watched people walking, driving, laughing and fighting. Then I bent down and took a handful of damp, dirty, dust in my hand. At that moment it occurred to me - the dust is where we all came from, it's what we all walk on every day of our lives and it is the thing to which we're all going back. If you think about it carefully, we never really did leave the dust.

ENVY NOT THE SILVER SPOON

Do not look at the man born with a silver spoon in his mouth and envy his fortunes above the wooden spoon in your own mouth.

For all you know, he too envies the great value of your wooden spoon - how he may use a little piece of it to pick out the meat from between his teeth, lest it decays and give his mouth a vile stench that denies him access to the king's presence.

Value is neither in the nature nor the content of what you have, but the use to which it is put.

LEARNING EDUCATION

Some things I learnt have added to me because they were the thinking of others. Some things I learnt have taught me to think for myself, I call the latter "education" and the former "learning". I love a man who is truly educated because his mind will sustain him; I admire a man of learning – if I should do anything more than like him, I may despise him.

EQUALITY IN DIFFERENCES

No one was ever created better than another was. We are all equal, not in our similarities but rather in our differences. There are none born luckier than others. Every circumstance you were born in was to give you an advantage, whether you are born with a golden spoon in your mouth or in the stable of a peasant farmer. Paradoxically, the latter is at destiny's advantage – for in the stable, he is blessed with both milk and warmth, whereas, the former may lack the suckling of the breast by virtue of the golden spoon in his mouth.

EVIL IS ALWAYS SITTING, WAITING

A Christian friend once told me someone else was evil.

"So are you." I said to him,

"How dare you!" He exclaimed.

"Well, you see," I said to him, "every man can be an angel or a devil. The excellent virtues I see in you are what makes you an angel to me, but the dark thoughts, hidden in the dark recesses of your mind - what you will do with such thoughts is what makes you the devil in waiting".

"Why do you keep me as a friend then?" He asked.

I smiled. "The very reason Jesus kept Judas Iscariot in His fold, yet knowing who he was."

THE TRUE NATURE OF A MAN LIES IN THE DEPTHS

Every being has evil within, yet a man by his excellent deeds and speech is considered good. His seasoned lips and gracious nature disguise all the wickedness of his heart and the evil in his mind. If it were not so, I would have perceived the rottenness of his soul a million miles away. What then – shall I say all men are evil? No! Nevertheless, seek to discern all men not with your senses but with your spirit. After all, I too am spirit and like the air he breathes, I will pass through his soul to see the depths that lie within him.

EXPERIENCE AT WORK

I was invited to sit in an interview. It was fascinating and I learnt something interesting: most people who claimed to have had ten years' experience, actually just have one year's experience that was repeated for nine years.

THIS THING CALLED THE REAL WORLD

There are and will always be two worlds – the physical world in which we live, feel and see things, and the very same world that exists but in our minds. Both are the same, one is simply a reflection of the other. So, what you believe in one world certainly exists in the other, whether you wish it to be so or not – It is outside your control. In fact, the only control you have is whether or not you believe a thing to be.

So, therefore, be careful what you go looking around for, whether in the physical world or in your mind. Surely, I tell you this truth, if you believe that gold and silver exist in your mind, it is merely a matter of time that you'll hold silver and gold in your hand. If you go about toying with the idea that a person is evil or good – it is just a matter of time before their good will become evil to you and their evil will become good to you. This happens all because of what you believe.

FAITH IS A SEED THAT GUARANTEES

Faith shows you a small seed and makes you see the big tree that it can become. Doubt shows you a big tree and the many fruits it won't bear. And so, I sit back and wonder why many will choose to doubt a thing – they do not understand that it is the seed first and then the tree, not a tree first and then the seed.

A man with faith only needs to see a seed to believe that it can become a tree that bears many fruits. But a man without faith needs to see the tree before he can believe that it can bear fruit with seeds in it. No wonder, it must be very hard for men without faith to see the greatness in themselves, much less accept that another man is deserving of greatness. After all, if we deem ourselves equal with all men, how can we accept that they have the right to greatness when we do not believe we possess such a right ourselves?

REALITY IN ITS TRUE COLOURS

I have two pairs of eyes – one opens into the world outside my being and sees what everybody sees; the other opens into the world within me and sees what nobody else sees in me but me. One is mortal, the other is eternal. Faith is not that difficult after all – I simply continue to see in my infinite mind, what my physical eyes cannot see. Do not only believe what everybody else sees? believe more what you see within yourself – for the latter is the true reality.

FAME IS LAZINESS THAT RESOLVES TO WORK HARD

Fame was never created to be found, it prefers to find you – but you must be doing something when it finds you, because it eats, drinks, breathes and lives on hard work. Its sustenance is not by laziness – it is work. Don't be deceived; fame is not for lazy folks. If you doubt me, ask the Messiah, Jesus. He called hardworking men into discipleship, not idle rulers sitting in royal palaces.

TO BE GOD IS FEAR THAT MUST NOT BE

When you shudder to go beyond yourself, when you struggle to rise above your current level, when you procrastinate in confronting your limitations – this does not come from your fear of the unknown or the abilities you lack or in the grace of heaven to support you when you doubt. What you really fear is the call to rise to become a god – you've simply been too busy being human.

KNOWLEDGE THAT LIGHTS A FIRE

A word just dropped in my spirit that the same FIRE that Paul used to warm himself in Malta was the same FIRE he used to destroy the serpent that attacked him.

Fire is a conflagration that produces light which is knowledge. This knowledge can be deployed for igniting revival or for ruthless destruction.

FRIENDSHIP

The only reason why a dog is a man's best friend is because it wags its tail, NOT its tongue!!

THE CERTAINTY OF OUR FUTURE

So many times people have said to me that the future is uncertain, and I have said back to them, "Well, to be very honest, the most certain thing about the future is that it will surely come. But what is really uncertain about the future is whether or not you are ready for it."

DIVERSITY, UNIFORMITY AND GLOBALIZATION

It appears the world's journey to becoming a global village has meant WE all feel the punches harder. But what's not surprising about a village, is that the impact it bears is always greater. Daily, the village is getting more crowded and we are losing our individuality that used to make the world diverse. Eventually, there really won't be a village big enough to contain all our inefficiencies or global enough to sustain all our volatility and greed. I am moving out of the village.

GREATNESS IS REALLY BELOW US

When I was a child, I equated a great person to be one able to affect a large number of people locally or worldwide; or one who has overcome great adversity in destiny's journey; or someone who was willing to die for a greater good. Then one day I asked myself: how about the poor peasant farmer, with no clothes on his back and no rest for his body nor sleep for his eyes. He battles the forces of nature and poverty to grow the grains that feed the bellies of such as we call great. His sweat-filled labour wrestles nutrients from the earth to sustain the health of those we call might – what about him?

Are they great also? For where does the great man stand with no food in his belly? How runs the mighty army that has no strength in their arms?

It is the ignorance of man that equates fame with greatness. The truth is – fame is merely a mass expression of envy. Few envy being a peasant farmer; if there were many who did, he would have much fame.

Fame is merely a mass acknowledgement of those we believe are better than our true selves. So, if we saw the peasant farmer as being better than us, we would have made him famous.

HUMAN RESOURCE MANAGEMENT
– AN UNUSUAL VIEWPOINT

Noah was in the Ark with giraffes, sheep, goats, kangaroos and other types of animals. Nevertheless, the journey was still good. In every institution's journey of evolution, no leader should expect to ride with only his people. In Noah's case, he didn't only ride with human beings, there were animals too.

You will always have more than "human beings" (*people of your KIND*) on the journeying boat. There will always be people on your boat who do not think like you, dress like you or be as diplomatic as you – just like the various animals on the Ark. But their being on the boat, makes the journey successful because, believe it or not, each one has its own contribution to make.

The sheep will provide the wool for clothing; the elephant's dung will be fuel for cooking and its trunk for fetching water. The kangaroo's pouch provides a means of transportation while the dove will be useful for mobile (satellite) communication.

Consider further that the parrot can become the means of ensuring that the core objectives of the Ark Company are perpetually repeated till they sink into the souls of all on board. The cock will be useful for motivating people to rise again after they have gone through the "night times" of their lives.

The owl that sees excellently at night will ensure that when dark times come, the entire company does not walk blind but rather, can still see clearly in the dark times – which are bound to come. The eagle, which is the only animal whose eyes can see 360 degrees, will ensure that the entire organisation has access to a 360 degree view of all available opportunities and foreseeable problems in the future.

Last of all, the lion will ensure whenever ruthless enemies arise along the way, they are dealt with decisively.

The greatest mistake any leader can make is to assume that everybody on his boat is a human being like himself, and as such, FAIL to tap into the unique abilities of each individual for the good of all. This is called HARNESSING your human resources, and if you cannot do this - you have NO business being a manager.

LAZINESS HAS A PRICE BEYOND US

"That was my idea! That was my idea!" shouts the lazy man, who takes no action! He thinks and dreams but does not act on it, so it remains exactly what it is – a dream. A vision received but not made manifest remains what it could have been – an illusion. And so also is folly – acting neither on your own thinking nor on the word of God, just acting. To do either is crimes against humanity, for both laziness and folly carry a price often not paid by the perpetrator alone.

GROW UP – NO ONE SAID THE WORLD WAS FAIR

People scream and say, "The world is not fair!" They speak as if it was ever created to be fair. The world only gives back what you give to it. Therefore, if you sleep away forty percent of your life and engage only five percent of your thinking ability, surely the world cannot be fair. You are being unfair. Failure and fortune are empowered to men – the lazy man is chosen by failure, the diligent man chooses fortune.

MY VERSION OF LAZINESS

I once heard a young man say, a lazy man was one who did no work; I said to him:

A man is lazy who doesn't sit to think when neither trouble nor anxiety presses him.

A man is lazy who doesn't strive to know himself and his abilities.

A man is lazy who will only dream and not act upon his dreams.

A man is lazy who will not do as he is told for his own good.

A man is lazy who has not yet embraced a purpose greater than his daily life.

A man is lazy who accepts no responsibility for where he is in life.

A man is lazy whose life has never poured out into another man's life.

LIFE IS A CRIME WHEN YOU STAND STILL

Life is always in a state of motion and so should you – either at the pace of life or faster than what is contained within life, if you can. Standing still is like being in the path of a roller-coaster – those on it and moving in tune with its speed will be having amazing fun and those in its path, getting badly hurt. Now you understand why I hate procrastination with a passion.

LIFE'S JOURNEY – FROM WITHOUT TO WITHIN

The journey of life is never to a destination outside of you. The destination is always to a point already within you. You'll ONLY become what you see yourself becoming WITHIN - that is the real destination.

The destination of life is NOT where we actually get to, it is where we start from – that is, from within! The truth is that the physical can never create the mental, but rather, the mental always creates the physical. This should tell you the real direction of life. Things flow from the creator to the created.

The real journey of life is to transport what's already within you to a place of manifestation in the physical, NOT to make what the world says you are into what you end up accepting within you.

It is a hard saying, but one worthy of acceptance as TRUTH.

IT WILL NEVER BE YOUR JOURNEY

Every one of us will walk a part of our journey alone and it is better that way.

Whether this is sanctioned by heaven so that we do not get distracted by those who would have wished we journeyed the way they did, I do not know.

What I do know, however, is this – whether you journey alone or with all of humanity, that journey is NOT yours alone. To those who see you at the start of your journey, you will be their inspiration that they too can walk it. To those you meet during the sojourn, you are their milestone – a proof they are not alone. To those waiting to see you on the other side, you are a prize that affirms their own journey was worth it.

Your journey is never yours.

A LIFE WORTH LIVING

You cannot guarantee life, but you can make it worth living. Approximately 153,000 people die every day. You could have been any one of them. The way I see it, that is 153,000 opportunities of life we each get daily.

What exactly are you doing with 153,000 opportunities? Some people get only one such opportunity and they work with their lives to bring glory to God. Some change the world by adding value to the lives of others, leaving a legacies for generations yet unborn. Yet still, others may do well to snatch a soul from the clutches of Satan for Christ.

If the sum of all your acts in any one day adds NO lasting value to yourself, another man, the world, or the generations yet unborn, then you have NOT lived – instead, you have denied 153,000 other people the opportunity to have lived your life and make something better out of it!

WHO IS COMING ALONG....WHO IS STAYING BEHIND?

By virtue of our very nature, one of the hardest things for us all is to recognize that there will always come a time when we have to decide whether to continue our journey with those we started out together with, or to leave them behind and move on. Here's the truth – if you know where destiny has called you to be and when you are needed there, you will know how to get there and who to go with there.

Beyond that, remember this: loyalty becomes insanity if a man who ought to run out of a burning city to get help stays in it and burns with all else in the name of loyalty. Why? Because in so doing, his loyalty has created neither an opportunity for saving anything or for preserving the history of the story of those to whom he is loyal.

LONELINESS – A CRY FOR INNER EXPRESSION

Loneliness can be joyful or painful and the cure for it is not in marrying or finding friends – after all, even relationships loneliness can be profound.

There are times you will be lonely because you cannot help it, there are times you must be lonely out of a necessity.

Loneliness is not necessarily the absence of people around you; on the contrary, it can equally be the hidden good in you, crying for expression.

Adam, the first man, originally had Eve hidden inside him, yet God said he was "alone" until Eve found expression on the outside of him – then he became complete.

LOVE – THE REAL DEAL

When it comes to LOVE, I do not have an awful lot to say. What I can say however is this: men may play the game, but it is the women who really keep the scores.

TO BE DEAD IS TO LOVE

This thing called LOVE: It is best to go into it as being dead first, and being alive afterwards. It will last this way. After all, being dead, you neither have expectations nor the will to hold back from giving what is expected of you. Paradoxically, I now understand why Jesus had to die first, in order to then exhibit his love toward us. For love's sake, die first, then live.

LYING ONCE, LYING TWICE, LYING LYING LYING

A man who lies once will feel he has fallen from moral grace. Then since it feels like there can be no further fall, being already down in the moral mud – so too, be believes another lie cannot make him fall any further beyond the mud. It's a paradox that such men are most troubled as to why everyone treats them like dirt – they forget that the moral mud has become their bed of roses.

WHERE THE BODY GOES, THE MIND HAS BEEN

Wherever my body goes, it takes my mind with it. Nevertheless, my mind by itself goes to places my body cannot go. It is not a matter of choice; no, it is a matter of the superior served by the inferior and the inferior bearing total allegiance to the superior.

Do not be deceived for a moment; it is not the body that leads, but the mind. Everywhere the body will go, the mind has already been. It is the same with the physical and the spiritual – you cannot hold in your bosom what you have not received in your spirit.

THERE'S JUST SOMETHING ABOUT SPACE

If you can afford space, buy, rent or otherwise possess it because it is a magic wand that helps a man think with creative inspiration. I used to live in a cubicle and so was my mind; then I created space and realized I had more room to think too. A mind that wishes to think big ideas must have a body that believes it has enough space to live such big ideas.

DO YOU REALLY THINK YOU THINK?

We are accustomed to think only when we have a need, when we encounter fear or when we have to survive a situation.

Successful people are those who make a conscious effort to think, often when they have no need or face no fear or challenges.

They simply think when nobody else sees the need to. Thus, they think of solutions before the rest of the world discovers the problem.

MAN, GROW THINE SOUL

A man has a brain, but without the thinking of the soul, he is nothing. He has much flesh but without the emotions of the soul, he is like corpse. The body can do nothing by itself. Oh foolish man, grow your soul also.

MODERNITY – SLACK HANDS, SWIFT EXPECTATIONS

I cannot understand why the minds of men grow feeble in accepting the truths that worked in the eras before us. They say to me "We are in a modern world." In truth, the only modernity I see is men whose hands are slack towards labor and who daily betray their souls to immorality. Life has become fast and without content – too fast to make meaning. This is life today – a bright colorful book with worn blank pages inside.

LIBERTY AND OPPRESSION ARE NEIGHBOURS

Every oppression emerges out of an attempt to find liberation from another form of oppression; every liberation arises from a cry to be free from all forms of oppression. None really exists without the other; and each has a life otherwise incomplete, without the other; none of these rules eternally – as long as we remain humans.

PERFECTION IN AN IMPERFECT WORLD

If you think about it, no one was born imperfect – God is not imperfect and creates none alike.

If you ask me, there are no imperfections, only a human mislabelling of God's perfections.

What you label a disadvantage will always remain to you, a disadvantage; what you call an advantage, though it seems imperfect, yet heaven and earth will find a way to turn it into an advantage.

Therefore, there really are no imperfections in any man. Even the Holy Scriptures say: "Be perfect for I am perfect"

Why would God set us an impossible task?

THE POSSIBILITY OF IMPOSSIBILITY

When you are young, to you, impossible and possible are merely the same – possible, only with different spellings. That's because you see things through the eyes of faith and creativity. As you grow old impossible and possible mean the same thing – impossible; that's because you see through the eyes of reality and prudence. Therefore, be wise and train your children to be wise also. Let the days of your youth be filled with dreams and visions, achievements and greatness.

FRAILTY AND POWER OF THE HUMAN MIND

On the train today, I sat by a woman, skinny, frail and simple. It felt as if the train was holding us in its belly like Jonah in the whale. I could not help pondering that this frailty of a woman was human, however, within her existed potential power and ability to make something much more groundbreaking than the very train she sat in. It made me wonder if as humans, we really are as weak as we appear to be. Maybe our real powers lie hidden in the unexplored parts of us – the very parts we fear to explore.

PROCRASTINATION – A GOOD TEACHER

There is such a thing called "TRADITION." I once thought of it as an evil warrior. I saw many good men and women bound by it in tormenting misery. I know of another such thing called "PROCRASTINATION." Contrary to what many say, it neither robs you of your time or your seasons. It merely takes politely, every unused moment you have no need for and embraces gratefully, every season you let lie fallow by your unproductivity. Perhaps, it is we who ought to learn from the shrewdness of this thing called "PROCRASTINATION."

THE EXPOSURES OF PROMOTION

Some people can never allow you to rise above them. It isn't because they doubt your abilities or because your rise is a threat to their own chances. It isn't because you are undeserving of it or that you have usurped their season. No – they simply fear that your advancement is what exposes their true level. When the times of promotion comes, grasp it, but do so away from those that call where you are rising from home.

PURPOSE

If a man identifies his purpose in life and fails to achieve it, I cannot find it in my spirit to pardon him – he is by every means, a successful failure. If a man however, fails to know his purpose and fails to fulfil it, I can forgive him. I am a fair man; I cannot fault a blind man for missing the door.

I AM HOLDING MY PEACE

Today, I hold my peace; tomorrow, my utterances will be filled with the silence of unblemished lambs; and in the years to come, the brightness of my unfolded destiny shall exonerate me. Then my accusers and those who took counsel against me by their lips and the voices of their prophets shall wonder and say: "Is this not him that we believed would have been broken?" And I will also ask them: "Did you not know that it was my God who had from the foundations of the earth declared my good destiny?"

YOU! GO AND ANSWER TO THE WORLD'S NEEDS

The world was created to be self-sustaining. The mechanism for doing this is quite simple – every man needs to identify his abilities, strengths, and talents and use them to give the best of himself to the world while here. If there is a need in the world that is not satisfied, a problem not resolved or an evil not ended, it is because someone is not giving the best of himself to the world. And I am sure that someone is not me.

WHY ARE YOU QUESTIONING IT?

If God gives a man a dream or if a man receives a purpose from God, it is because he is the man considered fit for the job. If you doubt it, ask God why He didn't choose you - you are just not wired for it.

INSTEAD OF A "THANK YOU"

I enjoy every aspect of my life, but nothing is more deeply fulfilling than when I give of myself to a fellow human being and when he comes to the realisation, that the only befitting response he can offer back is to say, "God bless you". It is these blessings that bring me true wealth – it is the only currency by which I can possess all things, even life.

READING OTHERWISE BITTER EXPERIENCES AWAY

If you can read, you have no reason to fail in life. If you remain unsuccessful after much relevant reading, it is your laziness that has done you injustice.

Nourishment is not necessarily how much a man chews but how much is absorbed into his being.

Understand this truth therefore: it is foolishness and much waste that you should strive to gain the experiences of life through your own bitter failures, when many before you have recorded their wasted lives in books, so that your simple reading can spare your otherwise bitter experiences.

TWO-WAY STREET OF REALITY

Reality is not a one-way street, but two. For with my eyes I see a thing and it registers an image upon my mind – this is reality. With my mind also, I create images in my mind that become physical manifestations – this also is reality. I will not judge which direction of reality is superior - from the physical to my mind or from my mind to the physical. Indeed, Christ was right when He taught, saying, "As it is in heaven, so let it be on earth" – as it is in my mind above, so it must be manifested on earth.

PEOPLE TELL ME TO GET A REALITY CHECK

The world embraces:
"Reality = Imagination - Creativity - Possibilities"

I rather prefer:
"Imagination = Reality + Creativity + Possibilities"

I am musing: this thing called "reality check"; does it only exist because there is such an opposite concept of "imagination unchecked"?

WHO KNOWS MY TOMORROW BUT ME

I once told a friend that I was very rich to which he responded with laughter.

"But I can't see anything, Marricke"

"You are right," I replied, "but indeed I am. The only difference is that you are looking at me now and I am looking at me tomorrow."

"How can you see tomorrow?" He asked.

My response: "Because my tomorrow was inside me from the day I was born."

AM I MY BROTHER'S KEEPER?

There is no right or wrong. The world was created perfect and remains so. Nature, as it is, has no wrong, no evil, and no imperfections. The world by itself is in harmony. Every wrong known, every evil perpetrated and every imperfection is the result of human relating to human – we are not each other's keepers.

In this truth lies the whole state of the world - whether good, bad, past or present. We are not our brothers' keepers. On the contrary, even nature, which has neither soul nor spirit, is its own keeper.

A WOMAN, IS ALL WOMEN

Men, when a womAn tells you to treat womEn with equality, she simply means, treat ONLY her with equality. When she says "womAn" it means her; when she says "womEn" she means her!

As such, when your woman tells you to be "very supportive of how womEn feel" - that call for support and warmth MUST NOT under any circumstances extend to your secretary.

SILENCE, THEY SAY IS VERY GOLDEN. IS THAT SO?

Silence, they say, is golden. Silence, they don't say can also kill you, if you're quiet for too long.

Truth is - the silent lamb and the roaring lion both believe that silence is golden. The only difference is - the lamb is silent when it is being led to the slaughter while the lion is silent when it is plotting to pounce on its prey.

It isn't mere coincidence that the Messiah is both referred to as a lamb and the lion of Judah.

THE SEEDS WE SOW IN SORROW

When a farmer sows, he digs to break the surface of the earth so his seeds may be planted therein. In times of sorrow, overwhelming troubles and grave discouragement, understand that the grounds of your life are being been dug and broken up for planting. The words you speak then, the emotions you encourage, the visions you allow your mind to see - they are all seeds; they will surely grow, whether loudly or in silence, whether visibly or invisibly.

OF SUCCESS

Being successful –

It is knowing why you are here,

It is knowing how you have been wired,

It is knowing whom you have been sent,

Then, delivering to the world the best of you intact, adding much, taking nothing.

TALENTS

Everybody comes into this world with a gift - some people just unwrap theirs early; some unwrap theirs late; and yet still, some end up unnecessarily admiring the packaging and never get it unwrapped!

TOMORROW IS SLAVE TO TODAY

Tomorrow will always be a slave to today. In today is hidden the future indefinitely. For in today I can sell the evil that was purposed for tomorrow or equally buy and keep the goodness that I find today, so I may enjoy of it in the future.

DON'T TAKE LIFE SERIOUSLY
– ONLY TAKE IT SERIOUSLY

Many people, even my beloved wife, have at one time or another told me that I take life too seriously.

"Well, well, well" I say to them, "I don't have the luxury of much time to accomplish all that I should. However, it is the least of my worries. My greater concern is this – my destiny, as I see it, is bigger than my own life and my life much more than the path on which it walks."

THE SWEET LIES OF TRUTH

There are people who lie, yet it sounds sweeter than the truth. There are others who speak the truth, yet it tastes bitterer than a lie should. It is really not about the truth or lie – it's the person telling it that makes it what it is.

WHAT IS RIGHT MAY NOT BE TRUE

That a thing is right does not make it true;

For a man to be of right standing, does not make his words true;

What is right or wrong is the fruit of man's judgment;

But TRUTH is one and TRUTH is God expressed.

THE BATTLE BETWEEN WILL AND CONSCIENCE

Truth is not the opposite of a lie.

In fact, truth is a conscious effort to bring your will in agreement with your conscience.

For your conscience may say one thing but your will may empower you to do otherwise.

I now understand why a man of good conscience will do all manner of evil – either his WILL hate's listening to his conscience, or he simply doesn't have a conscience.

THE THINGS 8 STRANDS OF GREY HAIR TAUGHT ME

I may not be fully grey-haired but I have learnt some interesting truths:

1) You cannot receive from God anything beyond what you are currently ungrateful for;

2) If you cast away the rock from which you were hewn, life will either hew out of you its pound of rock or give you raw earth to make your own rock.

3) Some people will never understand you; do not force them to do this. If you do, you are endorsing their misunderstanding of you.

WE FALL SHORT OF UNDERSTANDING LIFE

Life is so big that the closest we get to understanding it is to embrace our own distorted concept of what reality is.

However, reality as we know it, in itself is incomprehensible. It is dependent on our five senses and only the things our brains can fathom – but what about the things our brain cannot fathom. Shall we then ignore them?

That is what we have reduced our humanness to – dismissing what our limited minds cannot fathom as unreal.

Oh, how great the universe, and greater still is the awesomeness of its creator!

HOW COSTLY IS IGNORANCE

Do you reckon that wisdom is costly to get and that knowledge is expensive too?

Then, try ignorance – its price is much weightier than life and costlier than the pain of death. There is no disease comparable to it.

THE LEARNED AND COMMON MAN

Let the common man borrow wisdom from the learned and the learned man, common-sense from the ordinary man. They will both be fulfilling destiny and being a blessing to one another by so doing.

ALL THE PEOPLE YOU NEED – TO LISTEN, TO HEAR

It is not everything you ought to say to everybody; it is not everybody you ought to listen to. Howbeit, if you find one man who adds to your life by what he tells you and another who adds to your life by what you say to him – these two are all you need in life.

GIVING MEN WHAT IS EXCELLENT

Give a man an excellent thing, but do not give it for too long. If he comes back for more, he is under your control. If he does not, he has no discernment of what is excellent, so do not offer it to him a second time. If you do, he will look down upon you and consider you rather a beggar.

THE WISDOM OF POVERTY

More often than not, it is those with no advice to give at all who give the most advice; and those with the most advice to give who seek to have more of it. The poverty of men fills in them the space reserved only for wisdom.

Thus, by error, they too believe they rightfully ought to advise other men who are poor.

WHO IS THE WISEST IN THIS ROOM?

Between two or more men, it is easy to perceive who is wisest. It is usually the one who says a lot without talking much or one who listens much and asks more questions than he offers advice. If you meet such a one, consider yourself ignorant – then, you will be seen as truly wise.

I COMMIT TO YOU......

If he believes in nothing, he is lazy and slothful and to such a man I will commit nothing that demands accountability. If he believes everything, he is unstable and dangerous; to such a man I will commit nothing that requires his commitment, loyalty or discretion. I will flee far away from every man with such a disposition.

ITS ALL MY GOOD ADVICE

If I give a man good advice the first time and he uses it NOT, I will consider that he owes me nothing.

If I give a man good advice a second time and he uses it NOT, I will consider that he is perceptive to find his own wisdom.

If I give a man good advice a third time and he uses it NOT, I will consider that he has no wisdom at all.

If I give a man good advice the fourth time and he uses it NOT, I will consider that it is I who am foolish.

COMPARATIVE PRICING

Do you reckon that wisdom is costly to get and knowledge is expensive too? Then, try ignorance – its cost is much weightier than life and more expensive than the pain of death – and there is no disease comparable to it.

BUILDING TRUST

Give a man one toenail and if he scratches you with it,

Give him also your left hand; if he slaps you with it then do this –

Guard his voice from reaching your home,

And with your right hand, keep your lips from speaking in his hearing

SOME MEN NEED TO GET IT RIGHT

A woman comes into your life to be a perfect "HELPmeet":

(1) Only if YOU are doing something with which she can help you.

(2) Only if YOU are doing most of the work and not expecting her to be your workhorse.

Get up and LEAD and see if she won't follow.

Leaders don't spend half their energy reminding their followers who is the leader; instead, they spend it making an impact which becomes an overwhelming proof of their position.

WORDS – TO MAKE AND UNMAKE

Words are like arrows - by them a message is transmitted and by them death is delivered;

Words are like arrows - by them a kingdom is possessed and another, defeated;

Words are like arrows - by them the will of warriors enforced, the mysteries of kings deployed;

By words a man will possess a future yet unknown and preserve a season already lived;

By words all things are made present, by it all laws are established;

By words alone can a man fulfil his dominion as god in the earth.

IN THE LANGUAGES OF IMPERFECT MAN

I grew up learning my mother tongue and later in life, the languages of other men.

They both have two things in common. First, they contain words;

Secondly, words are never enough to describe the fullness of the heavens and the earth;

Speaking words forever means speaking the imperfections of man;

Oh, how I wish that my tongue were engraved with the writings of Hebrew.

WORK, HARD WORK AND ALL IN-BETWEEN

God "planted" the Garden of Eden and Adam was only required to keep it.

I am tempted to believe that when God drove Adam out of the garden, he had no choice but to plant his own garden and keep it.

I have often come across only two types of people – those creating their own world, and those merely maintaining the world created for them by others.

Perhaps it is essential, sometimes, that a man prays for God to drive him out of his garden of comfort – only then, perhaps, can he learn to plant one.

IN THE BUSINESS OF WORRY

Worry in itself is the only worry;

There's nothing created, that comes to us with the burden of worry wrapped around it;

It is man who chooses to worry. It never forces itself upon us;

The decision to be affected by a matter, to the point of worrying is not one made by "worry" herself – it is always made by us;

Sadly, worrying neither makes the picture brighter or darker - it only cracks the lenses with which we view life and its many blessings.

CHRISTIANITY

BEING ME

The sum of all my knowledge, of all I have achieved, of all I am and have been, when put together, will never compare to the yet unexplored power of God in me.

For the things that I am and the things I have been, that is just what they are.

However, the things I am yet to be are still a mystery - unfathomable.

My whole is not just, what I am; I am the known and the unknown.

Know me, not by what you already know about me alone.

THE BLESSINGS OF THE LORD

The world taught me that to be blessed is to abound in materiality;

But I am blessed with all spiritual blessings in heavenly places;

My true blessing is the grace of God, which is given to me daily to enjoy the breath of life and to have an understanding of His mysteries;

For this reason, my testimonies are not by virtue of what I possess.

Again, I say, He has blessed me with all spiritual blessings in heavenly places;

So that I can place a demand on heaven and as such, the thing that I was not, I can become and the things that I did not have, I can possess – by the blessing

MY BIG BANG THEORY

If you were brought into existence by the big bang, then you are the highest order of intelligence in that regime – only because a "bang" by itself has no intelligence, but you do.

After all, you can sustain yourself knowledgeably, but the big bang that created you cannot by itself.

Therefore, like God, you ought to be omnipresent, omnificent and omniscient. Why is it then that you cannot predict tomorrow from today?

Or does the anti-logic therefore not bother you – that the "created" (you) is of a higher order than the creator (big bang);

Perhaps, this theory is just what it says it is – a loud big bang – nothing more, nothing less.

CREATIVITY

Creativity in man is simply God's unfinished work at creation which He has deposited in men to bring to manifestation in due season. It is an indictment against a man's own destiny to stop God at work by virtue of his non-creativity.

DARKNESS & CREATIVITY

Every man lived in the darkness of a womb before birth;

Why then, do you tell me you are afraid of the dark?

It is so you'll remember that in every darkness, there is creation happening;

It is so you'll understand when the dark times come, so too come a time to build;

It is so when you are done birthing great things in the dark, you too, with the pride of God can say boldly, "*Let there be light*" – to reveal the works done in the dark.

This is the mystery of every dark season – it isn't created for fear, but for boldness, not for death, but to birth life.

DARKNESS: IT'S MYSTERY

(1) The hen lays an egg. If it broods over it, that egg becomes another living bird with the ability to reproduce even more chicks. If the mother does not brood, it turns out merely as an egg, served for food. But whilst it sits in its shell being brooded over, it experiences nothing but darkness. Yet in that darkness, it is being formed.

(2) Moses went to see God on the mount, but God came to him not in the light of day but in the dark clouds. Out of the very darkness of those clouds, God revealed to Moses all the books of the Law that now forms the basis of the entire Holy Bible – all within the dark clouds.

(3) The greatest practical victory of the death of Jesus was that first, He descended into the darkness of Hades to snatch away from Satan the keys of death and to release all those bound in captivity – out of dark, dark Hades.

(4) David was first anointed by Samuel and later called into the palace by Saul, yet his kingship was truly constituted in the dark dreary caves of Adullam where he hid with men who knew not where they were going – in the dark hiding caves of Adullam.

(5) Abraham had been blessed directly by God Himself, and yet it was only in the dark moment of Sarah's death; only in that singular most painful period of his life did he take the opportunity to buy with gold, a part of Canaan land from the sons of Heth. This was the very Canaan that became Israel's inheritance - in the dark season of his loss.

(6) God is God. He could have started creating the earth from any material He so chose, but there is a mystery why he chose to create all of creation when the earth was formless and DARKNESS was upon it – yes, when great darkness was upon it.

The DARKNESS you are going through is NOT created for weeping and wailing and anxiety or suicide. Your DARKNESS is the most fertile season for you to be creative and fruitful. Darkness was created for productivity and manifestation. When God said let there be light, He really wasn't now calling for light to be created, He was asking the light to now show forth the excellent things He was all along creating in the DARK.

DEATH FEARS ME, NOT I DEATH

The highest pinnacle of fear is death;

At best, you will overcome fear; at worst, you die;

Knowing that I will die someday is a forgone truth – a truth I have embraced;

Therefore, there really is no worse outcome anymore;

I, through Christ died once and it brought me glory;

Why then should I fear death?

Let alone anything lesser than death.

YOUR GREATEST ENEMY – YOUR GREATEST BLESSING

Life and death always live at the same address;

Because the thing that can bring you the greatest blessing is the thing to guard against most from destroying you:

Moses served as a prince, he learnt to use a rod for a sceptre; then as a shepherd for Jethro he used a rod for a staff; finally, as a leader of Israel he used a rod again for his godly authority.

The same rod he used to strike the rock in anger, which led his denial into Canaan. The very rod he mastered using....

David was a gifted strategist, endowed with grace to take over kingdoms and eliminate greater kings. The same gift, he unwittingly used to take over Bathsheba and eliminate her husband Uriah, whose blood spoke against his kingship. The very strategies he had so mastered...

Solomon was gifted with wisdom and excellent oratory - the same gifts that drew him to other bodies of knowledge and endeared him to many women, their gods and their destructive tendencies. Yes, the very wisdom given to him by God...

Do you think your greatest enemies are those who envy your gifts and abilities? No! Your greatest enemy is your greatest gift - the moment it stops serving the good of humanity and begins to rule you...

MY ENEMIES AT MY VICTORY TABLE

When I was taught to recite Psalm 23, I struggled reciting the verse - "He prepareth a table before me, in the presence of my enemies";

Well, the truth is, not all your enemies must be seated at the table the Lord prepares for you during your celebrations of victory;

Some must be crushed for the victory to be possible in the first place...

EVIL IN THE WORLD

We often ask why bad things happen to good people or better still: "Why does God let bad things happen to good people?"

In the past, in order to dodge the question, I have always responded by saying, "If you can tell me why God allows good things to happen to bad people, then I will give you the answer."

God set the laws of nature from the beginning of creation and will never interfere with them unnecessarily. So for example, the law of gravity dictates that if one good man and one bad man both jumped from the 9th floor of their office building, they will both fall on the hard road beneath and die. In the same manner, if they had both bought a lot of land in a waterway and built on it, when the tides should rise, both will have their houses destroyed by the floods. It's simply nature taking its course – and man has a duty to himself to understand and respect the laws of nature. Ignorance is no excuse; you will not be spared the consequences.

Secondly, God will never interfere with our "WILL" unnecessarily, and therefore, He will also NOT interfere with the repercussions of exercising that will. So for example: a Christian or atheist who fails to utilize his mental creativity or financial discipline cannot turn around and blame God for living in poverty. Neither can a youth go around having sex and expect that he has the covering of God, so everything will be alright. If God does not interfere with you exercising your will, don't expect Him to do so with the results.

Finally, in the eyes of God, no man is an island. So when He blessed Abraham, for example, He was actually blessing "a people" and when Adam was punished an entire "people" experienced it too. That's the more reason why we cannot live in isolation and say what someone else is doing does not concern us. You see, if you are an exceptionally moral person and corruption seems to be going on all around you and you stand back saying none of it affects you, very soon, your entire country will be listed as corrupt. This will include you, meaning that your own personal chances of winning international business contracts or exploring educational opportunities for your children abroad will be restricted. Yet you had said, "It doesn't concern me." It does. The blessings and judgments come upon us all!

A LIFE IN GOD

If a man cannot believe in his lifetime that there is a God, then he cannot also live the true essence of life. If he says his life is fulfilling, he has not only lied to himself, but his very life has been a lie because it has been lived deceitfully. In God is life and the essence of it. Every other thing is futility in disguise.

HOW CAN A MAN NOT BELIEVE

How can anyone say they have no belief; it begs disbelief. I cannot trust such a man for he has proclaimed himself omnipotent and high above all things. I know only one Omnipotent God, so the other must be a fraud.

GOD SIMPLY WANTS TO BE BELIEVED

I've embraced religions, kissed sciences, flirted with history and played with psychology. I've slept with philosophy and romanced the arts.

In all, I find this one truth – we humans are simply spending our entire existence struggling to understand the complexity of the world and all that's in it.

Maybe it is God's way of reminding us how omnipotent He is.

God does not want to be understood. He simply wants to be believed. Believe Him.

THE UNFATHOMABLE GOD

You DO not understanding God does not mean He does not exist;

You do not understand the air you breathe, yet it fills your lungs daily with life;

God does not want to be understood – He wants to be experienced;

How do you intend to understand God when you have not yet fully understood human beings who are His handiwork on earth?

We are on earth and God in heaven above – if we would fully understand Him, we must first understand everything that exists between heaven and earth.

HOW CAN YOU SAY SUCH A THING

How can you say you are a thinker without possessing the Spirit of God who possesses all creativity and knowledge?

How can you say you perceive a thing when your soul is dark with sin and light is not in you? What then do you perceive in your darkness?

How then can you claim to be a complete being when you have no union with God, who is the completeness of all things?

You tell me, how can these things truly be?

THERE IS A DEEP MYSTERY CALLED GRACE

God knew, in his infinite omniscience, that after His only son poured out His blood for our salvation, you and I would still be the humans that we are, save the redemption of our spirits....

Jesus knew the nature of Judas a long time before he betrayed Him. But he kept him around....

David knew Absalom, his tendency toward evil and his trickeries, yet he never applied his prophetic, wise, or combatant abilities against him...

Samson did not just know Delilah carnally. She had tried many times previously to take him down. But he kept her, faithfully...

Isaac named Jacob and Esau. He had prophetic insight from day one which of them would end up a bitter manipulator of the other, but he loved and kept them both under his roof....

The father of the prodigal son knew exactly how his son intended to spend his wealth, yet his heart was already prepared to take him back on his return - even before he left home.

They all knew the dangers they were exposing themselves to, yet they embraced it faithfully. Jesus was betrayed, David's Kingdom wrecked, Samson's destiny was aborted prematurely, Isaac ended life a broken man and the prodigal son destroyed the father's wealth and his brother's inheritance.

This is neither compassion, nor kindness. It is not empathy or sympathy. Did they all make a mistake embracing the very ones they KNEW would hurt them?

IT IS A GREAT MYSTERY..... and it is called GRACE

GRATITUDE – THAT'S ALL THERE IS TO GIVE

God has given me at least one reason to be eternally grateful to Him;

Every man ought to find a reason too.

He took me out of my father's house, and then I watched in awe as He blessed me and established me - a new order, a new bloodline. Who am I, O Lord, that you should bestow such marvelous favor upon me?

So great is your favor it bears a face I see daily and a voice I hear anew every morning.

In the darkest of my seasons, You created my crown and with the vileness of men's words against me, You have turned me into honey upon their very tongues.

I am grateful that no one else is God but You.

THE MYSTERY OF KINGS

If you'll seek after anything, seek to know mysteries. It will serve you beyond wisdom and move you above understanding. It is what turns peasants into kings and kings into gods. Seek to understand the mysteries of God.

MARRIAGE

Of marriage I say: every man, will come to the point where within his being, he knows he cannot live life all by himself.

It is the point where he feels a rib missing from his rib cage.

When he does, he should look closely around him, for he has just woken up from his deep slumber and God would have already created a woman fit for him.

I warn him though, do not look far, else you will stray onto another man's rib.

THE ECONOMY OF MONEY

The original Biblical term for the word "Money" is "Zuzim" which translates as "Movement"... No! It is NOT a mere coincidence!

Money, like the blood in any man, needs to be kept moving in an economy and in our own lives. As soon as it stops moving, the system that possesses that money dies.

Like blood, it must not be more or less than a certain quantity in the body.

If it is too much, there will be inflation; too low, and you have deflation and recession.

Blood cannot be increased by simply increasing the water or saline intake.

Blood MUST be increased by the transfusion of real blood, so too, you cannot increase money in an economy by artificial printing and indicator manipulations.

Money must be increased by the very underlying component of the "value" it represents – A MOVEMENT IN PRODUCTIVITY!

PRAYER & ALTARS

A day comes when you will have no strength to pray much less to fight.

The question is: do you have an altar that will speak for you, let alone war on your behalf?

Who would you empower - angels or mortal beings?

Answer me, and you'll tell by yourself whether your future is a weak or a strong one.

IMPURITY IS PURITY

The purest Gold is not that which has no impurity; it is one that has a little impurity;

The best vaccine or serum always has a little of the disease or poison it is to fight;

The best way to heal a traumatic experience is to return to the scene of the trauma;

Pharaoh's power over Israel was through his deities (serpents, lambs and firstborn sons) - the very elements deployed by Moses for the final release of Israel;

Satan tempted Christ by quoting Scriptures; HE overcame him using the scriptures;

Christ came to destroy sinfulness. He took upon himself sin, in order to cure it.

You want to solve a problem forever? Then the DNA of the problem must feature in the solution!

LOOKING WITHOUT AND WITHIN

They lied to us about the nature of reality. In the book of Genesis 13, Lot looks and sees the luscious plains before him and chooses them. These end up being part of the land of Sodom. After Lot left, Abraham stands in the same spot and also looks, but the Bible says he looks North, South, East and West.

What's the difference? Lot looked in one direction; Abraham took a 360 degrees look. But here is the fascinating thing - they both looked with their eyes. The truth is: Lot looked "without" and saw the restricted possibility (after all, your eyes can only see in one direction at a time); Abraham, on the other hand, looked within (imagination) and saw ALL the possibilities.

If you keep looking outside of you, to the physical possibilities, all you will see is failure, impossibilities, insurmountable competition, personal inability and a lack of opportunities.

OF THE SAME BEING – RELIGION AND SCIENCE

The conflict between religion and science is akin to that between married couples;

You should be careful what you say to them – they will most readily join forces to expose you;

There really is no conflict between science and religion. No, there is not.

They only exist together in duality just as we do as triunes.

Even knowledge has a body and a spirit – science is the body, religion, the spirit.

THE SERIOUSNESS OF LIFE

People have often asked me why I take life so seriously.

Well, my father told me something as a youth that stuck with me for good. He said "If you don't make it in life, you have not only failed yourself, you have failed the destinies of the countless people whose fulfilment of hangs on yours."

We are all interconnected. It is just the way God created the world. So, I have lived my life under two main principles:

(1) If any man crosses my path, they must remember that I was a meaningful part of their journey, and I must remember that I poured into them all that was in me which they needed for their journey;

(2) I may be able to answer why I did not succeed in life (God forbid!), but I can never answer why the destinies of many others that hung on mine failed.

Our lives are not just ours. Always remember, your actions could be the reason why someone out there may or may not see the fulfilment of life.

SIZE REALLY MATTERS...

A Sunday school teacher was teaching her class of children under seven years old about God. When she was done, she gave each of them a piece of drawing paper and crayons. Excited, they all got busy with their drawing as they were told. At the end of the session, the teacher inspected everybody's artistic impression of God until she came to Jason, a boy of about five years old. His paper was blank on both sides. The teacher, partly perplexed and partly curious, asked why this was so.

In his calm unruffled voice, Jason responded:" From what you have taught me about God, I really don't think He can fit on this paper."

What is the moral of the story?

The God who made us in His image is larger than life. So get bigger than everything life throws at you. Be large and in charge.

NO MAN HAS SEEN GOD……OR ME!!

No man has ever seen God. I could almost say the same about myself – almost!

Yes, you may have seen my body and caught a glimpse of my soul, but my spirit you will never see.

If God who is Spirit, you do not see and His spirit in me, you have not seen either, then indeed it is true – no man has ever seen God and no man has ever seen me;

Because the real me is my spirit.

THIS BEAUTY I DO NOT COMPREHEND

I share my thoughts with you. It is invisible, yet you say to me, "that's a beautiful thought!"

I show you a flower, it is visible and you say to me, "that's a beautiful flower."

How then do you perceive "beauty"?

How does the human mind comprehend things both seen and unseen?

Perhaps, it is not just about the word "beautiful."

Perhaps the human mind is both spirit and matter, thus sees beyond physical differences.

DO YOU SEE TIME?

Time is like a pod of beans with each bean, possessing the ability to germinate and produce further life, sitting in a SPECIFIC compartment of the bean pod. Our lives and the number of our years on this earth are like these pods – a stretch of time. Within that stretch of time are specific compartments of years, months, weeks, days, hours and seconds, and within those short or long time compartments, our destinies are held in little digestible bits, like bean seeds. When someone steals a 1-minute, or 1-hour or 1-day compartment of your time pod, they have also taken away from you, the destiny, opportunities and the life-creating abilities hidden in that time compartment. They are gone forever, never to be recovered.

Do you now understand why I treat time, in the manner I do? Time is NOT just money, time is life.

WOMEN MAKE LIFE BEAUTIFUL – DO THEY?

God created pretty much everything from His word or clay except one – woman;

He must have had a very good reason for going through the complicated processes of first extracting the spirit-cells, soul-cells and stem-cells of Adam's ribs, applying deep anaesthesia, and spending precious time performing ground-breaking surgery – just to make a woman.

What can I say? If you are worth that much of God's efforts and time, you are certainly worth everything – especially the diamonds!

I salute all women – both those in my life and those outside it. You make the world a better place.

A WOMAN AND OUR GOD

If you cannot honor a woman, you cannot honor God for in them is fashioned the very outcome of God's creativity and loving-kindness.

If you cannot live with a woman, you cannot live in God; for with them is the law of life exemplified – that what you sow in a woman, you reap, always and in excellent measure.

I bless God for the lives of our mothers, our wives, our daughters, our women-friends and our women-family.

WOMEN – THE GATEWAY TO UNDERSTANDING THE WORLD

I have no doubt in my mind now, that a woman is one of the greatest natural wonders of the world. I have been thinking about this all day and have concluded very boldly - if you can understand a woman, you can understand how the whole world works. Hypothetically, here is why I say this:

- Her ability to multitask could explain how all the complex components of the universe synchronize to sustain us all.

- Her intuitiveness could explain how our spirituality ought to enable us be in sync with God 24/7.

- Her regular and irregular mood swings could help us understand the climate changes and weather patterns.

- Her profound nimbleness in managing the home should teach us a lot about governance and business management.

- Her ability to cunningly keep her friends, in spite of gossiping with and about them as the situation may demand, without a doubt is the epitome of refined politics.

- Her warmth, dedication, love and extraordinary patience (sometimes) is a foretaste of God's love for us and His present help in times of need.

- Her inner and outer beauties and her unadulterated commitment to perpetually preserve and add to them should teach us how we ought to be jealous about our gifts and talents and the need to refine them.

- Her ability to cook wonderful dishes or, in some cases, not too wonderful dishes, is a lesson to us all to know that "real creativity" is in the process, not necessarily in the finished product.

- Her ability to conceive, birth and nurture a child reveals that in our lifetime, we all need to birth and give to the world as much or more of what has been deposited in each of us than the world has added to us.

....and now you ask me, where my wisdom comes from? Ha! It comes from God, who blessed my home with THREE wonderful women, from whom to deduce wisdom.
Isn't God a really good God?

AUTHOR'S OTHER WORKS

Title:	Is This Why Africa Is? (E-book & Paperback)
Description:	I ask all the questions about Africa that nobody else will. Deep, profound questions
Availability:	Amazon & Kindle
Link to View:	http://goo.gl/ecRMig

Title:	Where Did God Hide His Diamonds? (E-book & Paperback)
Description:	Discovering what exactly God has hidden in you, finding it & prospering freely from it
Availability:	Amazon & Kindle
Link to View:	http://goo.gl/ecRMig

Title:	Doing Business with God (E-book & Paperback)
Description:	60 shocking biblical principles for extraordinary leadership, business and politics.
Availability:	Amazon & Kindle
Link to View:	http://goo.gl/ecRMig

Title:	Midnight Philosophies (E-book & Paperback)
Description:	My Deep thoughts, Philosophies, Reflections – Whispers of my mind.
Availability:	Amazon & Kindle
Link to View:	http://goo.gl/ecRMig

Title:	This Godly Child of Mine (E-book & Paperback)
Description:	A revelatory book on how to raise godly children in a perverse and lawless world
Availability:	Amazon & Kindle
Link to View:	http://goo.gl/ecRMig

Title:	The Deputy Minister for Corruption (E-book & Paperback)
Description:	A Novel
Availability:	Amazon & Kindle
Link to View:	http://goo.gl/ecRMig

Title:	A Dove in the Storm (E-book & Paperback)
Description:	A Novel
Availability:	Amazon & Kindle
Link to View:	http://goo.gl/ecRMig

Title:	100% JOB INTERVIEW SUCCESS (E-book & Paperback)
Description:	A simple, straightforward guide to passing every job interview you attend.
Availability:	Amazon & Kindle
Link to View:	http://goo.gl/ecRMig

Title:	Bible-by-Heart (Mobile App)
Description:	A simple but effective App to help anyone memorize 500 Bible verses in a year.
Availability:	iTunes & Google Play Stores

Link to View:	http://goo.gl/T3UdPN (i-Tunes)
Link to View:	http://goo.gl/ljnECR (Android)

Title:	Holy Rat (Mobile Game)
Description:	An exciting Christian mobile game that unwittingly gets you addicted to the word.
Availability:	iTunes & Google Play Stores
Link to View:	http://goo.gl/bygjBi (i-Tunes)
Link to View:	http://goo.gl/F18RM0 (Android)

ABOUT THE AUTHOR

Marricke Kofi Gane, is a gifted African Author, Philosopher, Public Speaker, Coach and Educationist. His writings carry real depth, are highly motivating yet challenging every status quo. He displays dexterity of mind and refined humour where appropriate. He is never shy in some of his works, to show a strong balance between his Christian roots and the reality of living in today's world.

Discover for yourself, all that his writings stand for - to dare, to motivate, to impact!! For more on him, visit:

www.marrickekofigane.com

Dear Reader,

Thank you for reading this book. I am hopeful that the information provided in it has given you some new learning, challenged you, or provided some answers and inspiration.

I respectfully ask your indulgence in 2 simple ways:

1. Whatever positive action(s) this book has inspired you to take, DO IT NOW. Not later.
2. Help other potential readers who without you, may never read this book by simply following the link below to leave a review. It only takes 3 minutes, but it could be a lifetime blessing for someone out there.

   http://goo.gl/v03bu2

Thank you once again for everything

Marricke Kofi GANE

www.ingramcontent.com/pod-product-compliance
Lightning Source LLC
Chambersburg PA
CBHW061324040426
42444CB00011B/2763